CASTLES
WALES
AND THE WELSH MARCHES

THE NORMANS IN WALES

The castle was introduced into Wales and the Welsh Marches, or borders, by the Normans. William the Conqueror entrusted the borders largely to three prominent nobles – the south was granted to William FitzOsbern, Earl of Hereford, the central area to Roger Montgomery, Earl of Shrewsbury, and the north to Hugh of Avranches, Earl of Chester.

Though William I viewed the border area solely in terms of the threat from Wales, these nobles and their fellow Marcher lords soon expanded westwards, establishing castles as they progressed. The first castles were of the simple motte and bailey type, but as Welsh resistance hardened, the castles were strengthened and largely rebuilt in stone.

By the end of the 11th century, the Norman Marcher lords ruled the Welsh lowlands and borders virtually autonomously, but were unable to make much headway in the uplands, particularly in Gwynedd, the heart of Welsh resistance.

From 1092 Roger Montgomery made staggering advances into Powys, reaching the sea at Cardigan Bay and then sweeping southwards into Dyfed. After conquering Dyfed he made one of his sons, Arnulf, its lord and he built Pembroke Castle.

Roger Montgomery died in 1094 and was succeeded by his sons, first Hugh and then the capable but notoriously cruel Robert of Bellême, who was greatly resented by Henry I. His fall came first in Wales in 1102 and then several years later in Normandy.

From 1131 the Clare family, with Chepstow Castle as their base, founded Tintern Abbey and then began to expand remorselessly westwards. They reconquered Ceredigion and built at least nine castles, including Cardigan and Aberystwyth. However, the Welsh rebellion in the middle of the 12th century led by the princes Owain Gwynedd and Rhys ap Gruffydd overwhelmed Clare Ceredigion, and when the last of the castles, Cardigan, finally fell, Clare and Norman rule in Ceredigion came to an end.

The next generation of the Clare family was dominated by Richard FitzGilbert, Earl of Pembroke (1130–76), better known as 'Strongbow', who turned his attention to expansion into Ireland. The turning point for the family was the marriage of Richard of Clare to Amicia, eventual heiress to the powerful earldom of Gloucester. Their son, Gilbert of Clare (c.1180–1230), became the first Clare of Gloucester, which gave him control of Glamorgan. In the 13th century the Clares were the most powerful Marcher family, a fact spectacularly demonstrated by the building of the majestic castle at Caerphilly. But the male line died out when Gilbert, the 4th Clare Earl of Gloucester, was killed fighting the Scots at Bannockburn in 1314.

ABOVE: *Offa's Dyke was constructed by the Mercian King Offa in 784, as a line of demarcation between his kingdom and that of the Welsh tribes to the west.*

TOP: *A medieval manuscript illustration of David and Goliath depicts the latter as a Norman warrior, wearing a chain mail hauberk and carrying a straight sword and kite-shaped shield.*

EDWARD I'S CONQUEST OF WALES

In the early 13th century Llywelyn ap Iorwerth ('Llywelyn the Great') extended the territory and enlarged the power of Gwynedd, the centre of Welsh resistance. Welshmen from other parts of the country came to look to Llywelyn for leadership. After his death in 1240, his grandson, Llywelyn ap Gruffydd ('Llywelyn the Last'), emerged as ruler. The baronial movement against Henry III in England gave him his chance. In 1258 Llywelyn received oaths of homage and allegiance from nearly all the Welsh princes and subsequently styled himself 'Prince of Wales'. He ruled for the next 19 years with prestige and authority, in 1267 making the Treaty of Montgomery with Henry III, in which he was acknowledged as ruler of the greater part of Wales, but was bound to pay homage to the king of England. Llywelyn paid homage to Henry but refused to do so on the accession of Edward I.

Edward I declared war on Llywelyn in 1276.

ABOVE: **Gruffydd ap Llywelyn (son of Llywelyn ab Iorwerth) falling to his death in 1244 from the Tower of London, where he was imprisoned by Henry III. From Historia Anglorum by Matthew Paris (d.1259).**

BELOW: **The Norman keep at Cardiff Castle stands on a motte surrounded by a moat.**

He invaded North Wales in the following year, while other forces raised by the Marcher lords invaded Southern and Central Wales. Edward advanced in strength along the coast and then up the rivers, building castles where they dominated the valleys and could easily be supplied by sea. He surrounded Gwynedd, Llywelyn's power base, starving it into submission. Llywelyn was only partially defeated in 1277 but he was forced to accept a harsh peace settlement in which he forfeited half of his territory. When war broke out again in 1282, Edward and the Marcher lords used the same tactics. There was stout resistance until Llywelyn was killed and the Welsh cause collapsed.

Edward was taking no chances and expanded his castle-building programme. These castles represent the peak of medieval military architecture in Britain, with the principles of their construction, above all the mural tower and the gatehouse, reaching the height of their development. To build his eight castles, five of which were combined with new fortified towns, Edward had to mobilise a vast army of craftsmen and labourers from virtually every county in England. His most important recruit was Master James of St George, mason and 'engineer' from Savoy, who directed the building of several of the castles.

ABOVE: **King Edward I in Parliament with Alexander III of Scotland and Llywelyn ap Gruffydd: detail of a fictitious scene made up by the illuminator in 1534. From the Wriothesley manuscript in the Royal Library, Windsor Castle.**

THE RISE OF OWAIN GLYNDWR

The reign of Edward I had largely sounded the death-knell of Welsh independence, and English authority was symbolised by the imposing Edwardian strongholds. In the later Middle Ages they generally existed as centres of administration, where rents were paid, tenancies regulated, courts held and wrongdoers imprisoned.

This period of relative tranquillity was violently interrupted by the rebellion of Owain Glyndwr, a leading Welsh landowner who, in 1399, resorted to arms in his personal feud with the English noble Reginald, Lord Grey of Ruthin. This soon turned into a Welsh national uprising, with Glyndwr assuming the title Prince of Wales.

Glyndwr's strategy was to avoid pitched battles with the English and to try to reduce the castles by siege and guerrilla warfare. At the same time he sought to weaken the Lancastrian government in London by allying with the powerful northern family of Percy in the rebellions of 1403 and 1405 and with England's greatest foreign enemy, France. However, Glyndwr never really overcame the strategic problem posed by the castles. Their presence enabled Henry IV's gifted son Prince Henry (later Henry V) to crush the rebellion in the last years of his father's reign.

Glyndwr was able to capture Aberystwyth, Conwy and Harlech, but the English won them all back. He ravaged the town of Rhuddlan but failed to take the castle, while Caernarfon proved far too strong. In 1401 he attacked the castle with French help but lost 300 men in the process; he tried again three years later with up-to-date siege equipment, but was repelled by a garrison of only 28 men.

However, Prince Henry's sieges demon-strated the inevitable demise of the castle as the ultimate defensive weapon when his men dragged artillery pieces into Wales and did considerable damage to the fabric of the castles at Aberystwyth and Harlech. In Britain as a whole the castle had declined before artillery warfare had become really effective. Under the Lancastrians many royal castles had fallen into decay. In the later Middle Ages, some merchants who had grown rich on the wool trade signalled their national prominence by building castles, but in general the aristocracy increasingly viewed their residences in terms of comfort. The age of the stately home had dawned.

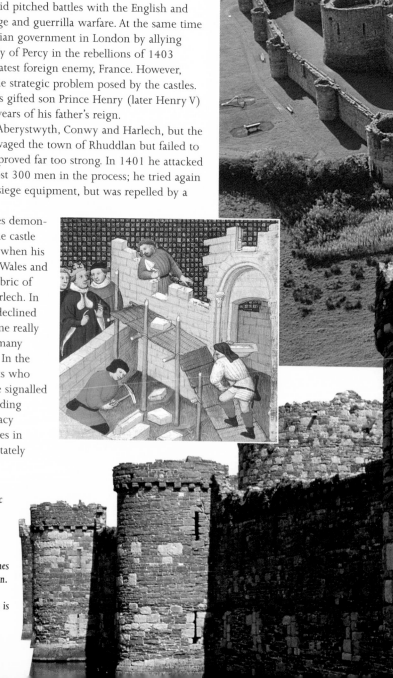

TOP RIGHT: *Beaumaris, the classic concentric castle in the British Isles and the greatest achievement of Master James of St George.*

ABOVE CENTRE: *A scene from a medieval manuscript depicting labourers shaping stones and building a castle under royal supervision.*

RIGHT: *The moat curtain wall at Beaumaris is punctuated by 16 towers and two gates.*

BEAUMARIS

At E of Beaumaris, Anglesey.
Open: SH. CADW

This concentric castle of almost perfect symmetry was the last and largest of Edward I's eight Welsh castles. Work began in 1295, under the direction of Master James of St George, and by 1298 over £7,000 had been spent and the castle was reported to be ready. However, though work recommenced between 1306 and 1311, the original design was never completed.

The inner ward is rectangular with a round tower at each corner, D-shaped towers in the middle of the east and west walls and massive double gatehouses with residential accommodation dominating the north and south sides. The outer ward is an octagon, having a drum tower at every angle except in the south where there is the dock and the Gunner's Walk, and an intermediate tower or gate on all sides save one.

CAERNARFON AND THE PRINCES OF WALES

Edward's son, the future King Edward II, was born in 1284 within the precincts of Caernarfon Castle and, according to legend, was presented to the people of Wales as their prince. In 1301 he was formally created the first English Prince of Wales and, at the same time, was endowed with the rule and revenues of the Crown's Welsh lands. From that time on the eldest son of the sovereign has customarily become 'Prince of Wales'.

In 1969, almost seven centuries later, Prince Charles was formally invested at Caernarfon by his mother Queen Elizabeth II as the twenty-first Prince of Wales.

ABOVE: The future King Edward II being created Prince of Wales by his father, King Edward I, in 1301.

ABOVE: The Eagle Tower at Caernarfon is built on a regal scale.

CAERNARFON

At W end of Caernarfon, Gwynedd.
Open: SH. CADW

Arguably the finest castle in Britain, Caernarfon was built by Edward I as the seat of his royal government in North Wales. The castle is a narrow-waisted enclosure incorporating in the upper bailey the remains of an 11th-century motte. It is bound together by the splendid series of mutually supporting polygonal mural towers, the most magnificent of which is the Eagle Tower, almost a keep in itself, combining the best accommodation with massive strength. The masonry is banded, imitating the walls of Constantinople. One of the two main gatehouses, the King's Gate, has been cited as the supreme British example of the immense strength of medieval fortification, incorporating two draw-bridges, five great doors and six portcullises, all covered by arrow loops and murder holes.

Work commenced in 1283 soon after the death of Llywelyn ap Gruffydd, but was violently interrupted by the Welsh uprising of 1294 in which the castle and the new fortified town were overrun. The King's Gate and the northern wall and towers were raised between 1295 and 1301 to strengthen the northern defences. However, as Edward became increasingly involved in Scotland, finances were redirected to his northern campaigns and in 1330 work ceased on the uncompleted castle.

The Queen's and Chamberlain Towers now house the regimental museum of the Royal Welch Fusiliers.

Caernarfon Castle, probably the greatest castle in the British Isles, is a fine testimony to the authority and building skill of King Edward I.

CAERPHILLY

In Caerphilly town centre.
Open: SH. CADW

Caerphilly Castle is a majestic sight, resplendent in its watery setting and fully reflecting the power and wealth of its lords, the house of Clare. Gilbert de Clare began construction in 1268 when Llywelyn ap Gruffydd extended his power south to the Glamorgan borderlands, but the castle was destroyed by Llywelyn in 1270. Undaunted, Gilbert began rebuilding in 1271, and work continued under his son, another Gilbert.

Caerphilly is a superb concentric castle. The inner ward is an irregular rectangular enclosure incorporating two gatehouses and four massive drum towers. The outer ward is a platform revetted by a low curtain wall. The castle is further protected by extensive water defences, walls, platforms, mural towers and buttresses.

CARDIFF

In Cardiff city centre.
Open (daily): Mar–Oct 9 am–6 pm;
Nov–Feb 9.30 am–5 pm.
Closed: 25 & 26 Dec, 1 Jan.
Tel: (029) 2087 8100.
City and County of Cardiff

Standing on a site originally fortified by the Romans, Cardiff Castle dates from the time of the Norman expansion into Wales following the death of Rhys ap Tewdwr in 1093. Robert Fitzhamon, one of the chief tenants of the Crown in Gloucestershire, occupied Glamorgan, and in the Roman fort built a timber motte and bailey castle which became the centre of a district administered like an English shire. His son-in-law, Robert the Consul, later utilised the existing defences and built the stone polygonal shell keep and the encircling curtain walls.

The great Clare family were responsible for developments in the following centuries, adding fortifications and dividing the castle into inner and outer wards by means of a great wall. Alterations continued at intervals until the wholesale restoration carried out by William Burges for John Patrick Crichton-Stuart, 3rd Marquess of Bute, between 1866 and 1881. The results of their collaboration are best seen inside the ornate Clock Tower, the Herbert Tower and the 15th-century Octagon Tower.

ABOVE: The west side of the flamboyant Cardiff Castle; from left to right, the Octagon Tower, the West Gate and the Clock Tower.

RIGHT: The ornate fireplace in the Banqueting Hall at Cardiff Castle depicts Robert the Consul, Earl of Gloucester, on horseback.

The massive and awesome Caerphilly Castle was built by the powerful Clare family.

ABOVE: *The handsome castle of Carew was equipped for comfort, with ample cellars and at least one fireplace in all the larger rooms.*

CAREW

On A4075, 5km (3 miles) E of Pembroke, Pembrokeshire.
Open (daily): Apr–Oct 10 am–5 pm. Tel: (01646) 651782. Pembrokeshire Coast National Park

This attractive castle stands by the River Carew, surrounded by meadows. Built on the site of a Norman motte and bailey structure between 1280 and 1310, it incorporates 'maisonettes' that were used by the chaplain and the constable of the garrison. The castle was extended considerably in the 16th century by Sir John Perrot, reputedly a son of Henry VIII, to create a comfortable residence.

CHEPSTOW

In Chepstow town centre, Monmouthshire.
Open: SH. CADW

Begun by William FitzOsbern around 1067, this was one of the first Norman castles in Britain to be built in stone. It dominated the main route over the River Wye from southern England into Wales, overlooking the river from a narrow spur. William built the rectangular keep, and a curtain wall, part of which has survived in the upper and middle baileys.

In 1115 the castle passed into the hands of the Clare family. When William Marshal held the castle in 1189 he built the wall which divides the middle from the lower bailey. His sons greatly enlarged and strengthened the castle with the remodelling of the keep (the Great Tower), and the addition of a barbican and the lower bailey with its very powerful double-towered gatehouse.

The castle passed to Roger Bigod II, Earl of Norfolk, in 1248. His son, Roger Bigod III, built the town wall and in the castle added the western gatehouse, the splendid Marten's Tower and the range of domestic buildings in the lower bailey.

The great Norman stronghold of Chepstow is dramatically situated on a cliff near the mouth of the River Wye.

ABOVE: Conical turrets give a fairytale air to Castell Coch, a marvellous Victorian fantasy created in the late 19th century.

CASTELL COCH

Off the A470 at Tongwynlais, 9km
(6 miles) NW of Cardiff.
Open: SH. CADW

In the 1870s, on the site of a ruined medieval stronghold, William Burges designed and constructed for the 3rd Marquess of Bute the delightful, fairy-tale Castell Coch, a masterpiece of Victorian medievalism. The walls, ceilings, doorways, fireplaces and furnishings are all carved, painted, gilded and often embellished with mythological and biblical figures, butterflies, animals, plants and stars.

CHIRK

Off A5, 1.5km (1 mile) W of Chirk, Wrexham.
Open: Apr–Oct, daily except Mon & Tues (but open Bank
Holiday Mons, & Tues in July & Aug) 11 am–5 pm (4 pm in
Oct); grounds 10 am–6 pm. Open some winter weekends -
ring to enquire. Tel: (01691) 777701. The National Trust

This important Edwardian border stronghold dating
from about 1295 occupies a prominent hilltop site. The
castle changed hands with regularity until, in 1595, it
was purchased by Sir Thomas Myddelton, a merchant
adventurer. It remained the
property of his family until
1978 when it passed to The
National Trust. A stately
home of great elegance and
style, it is sumptuously
furnished with paintings,
furniture and objets d'art
and stands in some of
Wales' finest countryside.

RIGHT: *Beautiful gardens surround
Chirk Castle, now a stately home.*

ABOVE: *At the entrance to Chirk Castle is a pair
of particularly fine elaborate iron gates, made by
the celebrated Davies brothers in 1719–21.*

BELOW: *The towers of the barbican wall at
Chepstow Castle have defensive arrow-slits.*

CILGERRAN

Off A478, 5km (3 miles) S of Cardigan,
Pembrokeshire.
Open (daily):
Apr–Oct 9.30 am–6 pm;
Nov–Mar 9.30 am–4 pm. CADW

This powerful stone castle, dating from the early 13th century, is dramatically positioned on a rocky promontory overlooking the gorge of the River Teifi. It was reputedly from Cilgerran that Nest, the beautiful wife of Gerald of Windsor, was kidnapped by Owain, son of the Prince of Powys, in 1109.

ABOVE: *Much of Cilgerran Castle was built by William Marshall the younger.*

CONWY

In Conwy town, Aberconwy & Colwyn. Open: SH. CADW

The picturesque walled town of Conwy is dominated by the towers and battlements of Edward I's famous castle, built following the completion of his conquest of Gwynedd. The castle was begun in 1283 and, under the direction of Master James of St George, was substantially completed in only 4^{1}/$_{2}$ years. The town's walls, which were built at the same time as the castle in a single defensive unit, constitute one of the best-preserved and most extensive urban defences in Britain.

The castle is built to a linear plan, irregularly shaped to fit the rock site upon which it stands, and is divided into two separate wards by a cross wall. The eight mural drum towers are massive in their strength and contain the best domestic suites.

ABOVE: *The inner ward, at the heart of Conwy Castle, was occupied by the private apartments of the king and queen.*

King Edward I's powerful castle at Conwy was begun in 1283 and virtually completed in 4¹/₂ years.

CRICCIETH

On hill overlooking Criccieth,
Gwynedd.
Open SH; open site at all other times.
CADW

The ruins of Criccieth Castle, which stand dramatically on a high promontory overlooking the town and the sea, incorporate both Welsh and English remains. The Welsh castle, in existence in the early 13th century, was occupied by Edward I's armies in 1283. The 'English' castle was completed by 1292 and, supplied by sea from Ireland, withstood the Welsh rising of 1294–5 with a garrison of about 20 men. Repairs and additions were carried out in the 14th century but in 1404 the castle surrendered 'from hunger and despair' to Owain Glyndwr, and was left gutted and ruined.

RIGHT: *The ruins of Criccieth Castle occupy a rocky promontory that juts out into Tremadog Bay.*

BELOW: In 1645, during the Civil War, King Charles stayed at Denbigh Castle for three days.

DENBIGH

Overlooking Denbigh, Denbighshire.
Open: Apr–Oct, daily 10 am–5 pm;
open site at other times in winter. CADW

Henry de Lacy, Earl of Lincoln, built this castle on a hill dominating the Vale of Clwyd, on the orders of Edward I. Work began in 1282, under the guidance of Master James of St George, and the southern and western walls, with their semicircular towers, were raised.

During the Welsh revolt of 1294 the castle fell, but was recovered by the English after the collapse of the rebellion. More defences were built at this time, including the impressive Great Gatehouse, consisting of three octagonal towers in triangular formation. De Lacy died in 1311, but it is traditionally believed that he stopped work on the castle when his eldest son, Edmund, fell into the castle well and drowned. Further building was carried out in the 14th and 15th centuries.

FLINT

On A548, 16km (10 miles) NW of Chester, Flintshire.
Open: all reasonable hours. CADW

Work on Edward I's first great Welsh fortification began at Flint in July 1277 and continued until 1286, combining a castle and a town in one defensive unit. The castle is built on a low promontory bordering the shores of the River Dee. The outer bailey has now almost disappeared. The powerful inner bailey is more or less rectangular with three angle drum towers and the dominating Great Tower.

ABOVE: Flint Castle was originally surrounded by water, and was attached to a town built to accommodate English settlers.

ABOVE INSET: This early 15th-century French manuscript illustrates the arrest at Flint Castle of Richard II by Henry Bolingbroke in 1399, following which Henry proclaimed himself the first Lancastrian king of England.

GOODRICH

Off A40, 6km (4 miles) SW of Ross-on-
Wye, Hereford & Worcester.
Open (daily): Mar–May & Sep–Oct
10 am–5 pm; Jun–Aug 10 am–6 pm;
Nov–Feb 10 am–4 pm (except T & W)
Closed: 24–26 Dec, 1 Jan. Tel: (01600)
890538. English Heritage

The castle stands on a high spur on
the bank of the River Wye. Its earliest surviving work is the square
keep, probably dating from the
middle of the 12th century. In the
early 13th century a square stone
curtain wall with angle towers was
added. The rectangular inner ward,
powerful gatehouse and three angle
drum towers were probably built
by Henry III's half-brother William
de Valence, Earl of Pembroke.

ABOVE: *A 12th-century square keep dominates the great Marcher stronghold at Goodrich.*

*When Harlech Castle was built, the sea came right up to the rocky
outcrop on which the castle stands, giving it a strong defensive position.*

HARLECH

On A496, 17km (11 miles) N of Barmouth,
Gwynedd. Open: SH. CADW

Edward I's powerful Harlech Castle is
dramatically positioned on a rocky promontory between the sea and the mountains of
Snowdonia. Concentric in plan, it is a
masterly achievement of medieval military
architecture. Work on the castle began in
1283 under the direction of Master James
of St George, and, at times employing nearly
950 men, was completed in 1289.

The main inner ward is a quadrangle
surrounded by a powerful curtain wall with
four massive drum towers. The dominating
Great Gatehouse incorporates three double-
leaved wooden gates and three portcullises,
all covered by arrow loops and murder holes.
A lower outer curtain wall gives a rather
constricted concentric outer ward.

The provision of supply by sea enabled
Harlech to hold out in the rebellion of 1294,
but, with the help of a blockading French
fleet, the castle fell to Owain Glyndwr in
1404. The future King Henry V recaptured it
several years later. In the middle of the 15th
century Harlech played a prominent part in
the Wars of the Roses, holding out against the
Yorkists for seven years, the longest recorded
siege in Britain.

KIDWELLY

Near Kidwelly town centre, Carmarthenshire. Open: SH. CADW

One of several Norman castles built along the coastal plain of South Wales, Kidwelly is positioned at the head of an estuary, thus ensuring naval supply. The first castle was built in earth and timber by Roger of Salisbury around 1106, but the earliest surviving masonry work is the rectangular inner ward, erected in about 1275.

The construction of a new hall, the chapel and kitchen followed around 1300, when the castle had passed into the hands of the House of Lancaster. The stone outer defences were added a little later in the 14th century. As the outer curtain wall was higher than the original timber defences, the towers of the inner ward had to be heightened in order to command the outer defences. The Great Gatehouse was probably finished by Henry IV in 1401 and was repaired following damage in the siege of 1403 by Glyndwr's rebels.

ABOVE: Kidwelly is one of the most well preserved castles in Wales. Its early 14th-century chapel projects outwards from the curtain wall high above the River Gwendraeth.

RIGHT: Kidwelly Castle's massive 14th-century gatehouse has three murder hole arches near the top.

LUDLOW

Ludlow town centre, Shropshire.
Open (daily): Apr–Jul & Sep 10 am–5 pm;
Aug 10 am–7 pm; Oct–Mar 10 am–4 pm.
Closed: 25 Dec and weekdays in Jan.
Tel: (01584) 873355. Privately owned

This 11th-century castle was founded by the Lacy lords from Lassy (Calvados) in Normandy. It was built in stone, with a walled enclosure incorporating mural towers, and a gate-tower that was converted into a keep during the 12th century. The inner ward contains the circular nave of the 12th-century chapel.

Dating from the 14th century, when the castle was held by the Mortimers, are the great hall, the domestic buildings of the inner ward and Mortimer's Tower in the great outer ward. The 16th- and 17th-century work marks the castle's later role as the headquarters of the Council of the Marches.

MANORBIER

Off A4139, 8km (5 miles) SW of Tenby, Pembrokeshire.
Open (daily): Easter–Sep 10.30 am–5.30 pm.
Tel: (01834) 871394. Privately owned

Gerald of Wales (Giraldus Cambrensis) was born at Manorbier Castle in about 1146. The famous churchman, courtier and man of letters later wrote of his beloved home, 'the castle … is excellently well defended by turrets and bulwarks, and is situated on the summit of a hill … having on the northern and southern sides a fine fish pond under its wall … and a beautiful orchard on the same side'.

Manorbier has survived as a powerful reminder of Norman military architecture. The stone castle, constructed in the 12th century by the de Barri family, replaced an earlier wooden structure. It was later fortified against Owain Glyndwr and saw action in the English Civil War.

ABOVE: *The great Marcher castle at Ludlow is perched on a cliff above the Teme Valley.*

ABOVE: Manorbier Castle, the ancestral residence of the de Barri family, was described by Giraldus Cambrensis as 'the pleasantest spot in Wales'.

RIGHT: The 14th-century domestic buildings and the round nave of the 12th-century chapel in the inner ward at Ludlow Castle.

Pembroke Castle, within its tidal moat, is dominated by an impressive late 12th-century domed keep.

BELOW: The extravagant Victorian mansion of Penrhyn was designed by Thomas Hopper in the style of a Norman castle.

ABOVE: The State Bedroom at Penrhyn Castle contains a massive carved oak bed, designed by Thomas Hopper.

PEMBROKE

In Pembroke town, Pembrokeshire.
Open (daily): Apr–Sep 9.30 am–6 pm, Mar & Oct 10 am–5 pm,
Nov–Feb 10 am–4 pm. Closed 24–26 Dec & 1 Jan.
Tel: (01646) 681510. Privately owned

Pembroke Castle was first built in 1093 by Arnulf Montgomery, who placed it in the custody of Gerald of Windsor. In the course of the 12th century it was strengthened and enlarged, making it one of the most important Norman strongholds in Wales. The castle passed into the hands of the Clare family and was used by 'Strongbow' (Richard FitzGilbert, Earl of Pembroke) as his base during the Irish wars.

When he died in 1176, leaving only a daughter, the castle passed to the Crown. Henry II later arranged for the heiress to be married to William Marshall in 1189. In about 1200, William built the splendid and dominating circular great tower with its spiral staircase within and two concentric fighting galleries around and upon it. Beneath the castle is the remarkable Stone Age Wogan cavern.

ABOVE: *A view along the Fuschia Arch in the garden at Penrhyn Castle.*

PENRHYN

Off A55, just E of Bangor, Gwynedd.
Open (daily except Tue): Apr–Jun, Sep & Oct 12 noon–5 pm (grounds 11 am–5 pm);
Jul & Aug 11 am–5 pm (grounds 10 am–5 pm).
Tel: (01248) 353084. The National Trust

Penrhyn Castle is an outstanding example of Regency neo-Norman architecture, set in the midst of beautiful gardens and wooded parkland. It was designed and built for G.H. Dawkins Pennant in the early 19th century by Thomas Hopper, using Anglesey marble and other local materials wherever possible, and passed to The National Trust in 1951. Notable features of the building are the hot-air heating system, the water closets and the original furnishings. Penrhyn also has a first-class industrial railway museum and more than 1,000 dolls dating from the early 19th century.

The view from the Orangery Terrace at Powis
Castle, looking south-east towards England.

POWIS

Off A483/A490, 1.5km (1 mile) S of Welshpool, Powys. Open: castle (daily except Tue & Wed) Apr–Sep 1 pm–4 pm, open Weds in July & Aug. Garden: as for castle and weekends in Nov; Apr–Sep 11 am–5.30 pm, Oct 11 am–5 pm, Nov 10 am–3 pm. Tel: (01938) 551929. The National Trust

Powis Castle, the seat of the princes of Upper Powys in the 13th century, was destroyed by Llywelyn ap Gruffydd in 1275, but following the Edwardian conquest was rebuilt by Gruffydd ap Gwenwynwyn after he had agreed to drop his princely title.

The rooms today contain many treasures, including Flemish tapestries, paintings and a large variety of antique furniture. In front of the castle are picturesque gardens laid out in the 18th century.

RAGLAN

On A40, 11km (7 miles) SW of Monmouth, Monmouthshire. Open: SH. CADW

Raglan Castle dates from the 15th century and the rise of Sir William ap Thomas, a veteran of the French wars. The ultimate defence is the Great Tower, surrounded by water and originally approached only by a drawbridge. Thomas's son Sir William Herbert, Earl of Pembroke, probably made the largest contribution to the buildings, his principal works being Fountain Court, Pitched Stone Court and the Great Gate.

ABOVE: *Powis Castle was once a major border stronghold and still boasts a much altered medieval gatehouse and keep.*

Raglan Castle's hexagonal five-storey Great Tower is surrounded by a water-filled moat, and was connected to the rest of the castle by a drawbridge.

RHUDDLAN

On A547, 5km (3 miles) S of Rhyl, Denbighshire.
Open (daily): 18 Apr–24 Sep 10 am–5 pm. CADW

Since the 8th century Rhuddlan has figured promi-
nently in the continual border struggles between
England and Wales. A motte and bailey castle was
raised by Robert of Rhuddlan in 1073.

In 1277 Edward I advanced to Rhuddlan, where
Llywelyn, Prince of Wales, submitted to him. The inde-
fatigable Master James of St George oversaw the building of the new castle, which was completed by 1282.
A new channel was dug for the River Clwyd so that
the castle had deep water access from the sea.
Rhuddlan castle is concentric in plan. The perfectly
symmetrical inner ward has two great drum towers
and two massive double-towered gatehouses.

ABOVE: *Rhuddlan Castle, raised by Edward I following his first
campaign in Wales, stands on the site once occupied by an Anglo-
Saxon settlement called Cledemutha.*

ABOVE: *Within the walls of an abandoned medieval castle stands
St Fagans, a large Elizabethan mansion, which now houses extensive
collections illustrating Welsh life and culture.*

ST FAGANS CASTLE
and National History Museum

W of Cardiff, off M4 Junction 33.
Open: daily 10 am–5 pm and Bank Hol Mons
Closed: 24 & 25 Dec.
Tel: (029) 2057 3500. National Museums and Galleries of Wales

This 13th-century castle houses an attractive mansion
constructed during the reign of Elizabeth I by Dr John
Gibbon. It is now the home of the National History
Museum and the rooms have been restored and
furnished to represent the castle as it was at the end of
the 19th century. In the grounds there are a number of
re-erected buildings, including a working woollen mill,
wood-fired bakery, school, smithy and farmhouses.

STOKESAY

On A49, 11km (7 miles) NW of Ludlow, Shropshire.
Open: Apr–Sep, daily 10 am–5 pm; Oct, Wed–Sun 10 am–5
pm; Nov–Feb, Wed–Sun 10 am–4 pm; Mar, Wed–Sun 10 am–
5 pm. Closed: 24–26 Dec.
Tel: (01588) 672544. English Heritage

Stokesay Castle is one of the best surviving examples of
a fortified manor house. In about 1240 the Say family
built the two lower storeys of the north tower, and in
about 1281 it was purchased by the richest wool
merchant in the realm, Lawrence of Ludlow. Ludlow
demolished the older buildings and constructed the
present hall, solar block, south tower and almost
vanished curtain wall. The work was probably
completed by the early 14th century.

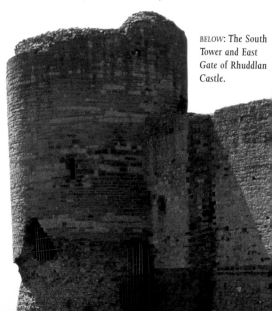

BELOW: *The South
Tower and East
Gate of Rhuddlan
Castle.*

ABOVE: The fortified manor house at Stokesay dates from the 13th century.

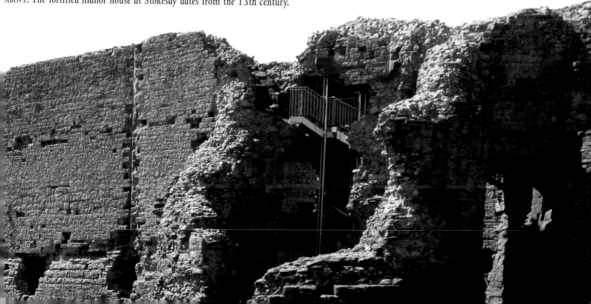

The 'Three Castles':
GROSMONT, SKENFRITH AND WHITE

Distance NW of Monmouth, Monmouthshire: Grosmont: on B4347, 16km (10 miles); Skenfrith: on B4521, 12km (8 miles); White: off B4233, 16km (10 miles).
Open: Grosmont and Skenfrith: open site; White: Apr–Sep, daily 10 am–5 pm; Oct–Mar, open site. CADW

These three castles form the 'Monmouthshire Trilateral'. In 1201 King John granted them to Hubert de Burgh, an officer in the royal service. He forfeited them in 1204 when he became a prisoner of war in France, and it was not until 1219 that he regained them.

Of particular note are the remains of the large first-floor hall at Grosmont, the powerful cylindrical keep at Skenfrith and the gatehouse at White Castle.

TOP RIGHT: The castle of Grosmont stands on the motte (or gros mont – big hill) where an earlier, Norman castle once stood.

LEFT: A chessman dating from the 12th–13th century, found at Skenfrith Castle, now at the National Museum and Gallery, Cardiff.

CENTRE RIGHT: Skenfrith Castle was built at an important crossing point of the River Monnow.

BELOW: Traces of the white plaster rendering that once covered White Castle's walls and towers, and from which the castle's name derives, can still be seen.

ABOVE: The massive cylindrical Great Tower dominates Tretower Castle in the beautiful Usk Valley.

TRETOWER

On A479, 15km (9 miles) NW of Abergavenny, Powys.
Open (daily): March 10 am–4 pm; Apr–Sept 10 am–5 pm;
Oct 10 am–4 pm. Closed in 2009. CADW

Tretower Castle is dominated by its splendid early 13th-century circular tower, constructed on a Norman motte and within a 12th-century shell-keep. The tower has three storeys with a basement, its entrance is at first-floor level and its walls are three metres (nine feet) thick. The castle, founded by the Norman Knight Picard, was held by the Picard family until the early 14th century.

Near the castle lies Tretower Court, a later medieval manor house and for three centuries the residence of the Vaughan family. The earliest building is the north range, with masonry from the 14th century.

OTHER CASTLES IN WALES
AND THE WELSH MARCHES

Most of the castles below are normally open to visitors.

CADW Welsh Historic Monuments
Beaupre, nr Cowbridge, Vale of
  Glamorgan
Carreg Cennen, nr Llandeilo,
  Carmarthenshire
Castell y Bere, Abergynolwyn,
  Gwynedd
Coity, Bridgend
Dinefwr, Llandeilo,
  Carmarthenshire
Dolbadarn, Llanberis, Gwynedd
Dolforwyn, Abermule, Powys
Dolwyddelan, Gwynedd
Dryslwyn, nr Llandeilo,
  Carmarthenshire
Ewloe, nr Hawarden, Flintshire
Laugharne, Carmarthenshire
Llansteffan, Carmarthenshire
Llawhaden, Pembrokeshire
Loughor, Swansea
Monmouth, Monmouthshire
Montgomery, Powys
Newcastle, Bridgend
Newport, Newport
Ogmore, Bridgend
Oxwich, Swansea
Swansea, Swansea
Weobley, Swansea

English Heritage
Acton Burnell, Shropshire
Beeston, Cheshire
Chester, Cheshire
Clun, Shropshire
Longtown, Hereford & Worcester
Moreton Corbet, Shropshire
Wigmore, Hereford & Worcester

Others
Abergavenny, Monmouthshire
Aberystwyth, Ceredigion
Barry, Vale of Glamorgan
Brecon, Powys
Bryn Brâs, Llanrug, Gwynedd
Builth, Builth Wells, Powys
Caergwrle, Flintshire
Caldicot, Monmouthshire
Candleston, Bridgend
Cardigan, Ceredigion
Carmarthen, Carmarthenshire
Crickhowell, Powys
Deganwy, Aberconwy & Colwyn
Dinas Brân, Llangollen,
  Denbighshire
Dyserth, Denbighshire
Ewyas Harold, Hereford & Worcester
Haverfordwest, Pembrokeshire

Hawarden, Flintshire
Hay, Hay-on-Wye, Powys
Hereford, Hereford & Worcester
Holt, Wrexham
Llandovery, Carmarthenshire
Morlais, Merthyr Tydfil
Neath, Neath & Port Talbot
Newcastle Emlyn, Carmarthenshire
Oystermouth, Swansea
Pembridge, Hereford & Worcester
Penhow, Newport
Pennard, Swansea
Penrice, Swansea
Picton, Pembrokeshire
Richard's, nr Ludlow, Hereford &
  Worcester
Roch Castle, nr Haverfordwest,
  Pembrokeshire
Ruthin, Denbighshire
Shrewsbury, Shropshire
Tenby, Pembrokeshire
Usk, Monmouthshire
Wilton, Bridstow, Hereford &
  Worcester

Llansteffan Castle stands on the site of an Iron Age fort, overlooking the Tywi estuary.